Please visit our website, www.garethstevens.com. For a free color catalog of all our high-quality books, call toll free 1-800-542-2595 or fax 1-877-542-2596.

Cataloging-in-Publication Data

Names: Claybourne, Anna.
Title: Messy experiments / Anna Claybourne.
Description: New York : Gareth Stevens Publishing, 2019. | Series: Ultimate science lab | Includes glossary and index.
Identifiers: ISBN 9781538235348 (pbk.) | ISBN 9781538235362 (library bound) | ISBN 9781538235355 (6pack)
Subjects: LCSH: Science--Experiments--Juvenile literature.
Classification: LCC Q164.C5725 2019 | DDC 507.8--dc23

First Edition

Published in 2019 by
Gareth Stevens Publishing
111 East 14th Street, Suite 349
New York, NY 10003

Copyright © Arcturus Holdings Ltd, 2019

Author: Anna Claybourne
Science consultant: Thomas Canavan
Experiment illustrations: Jessica Secheret
Other illustrations: Richard Watson
Photos: Shutterstock
Design: Supriya Sahai, with Emma Randall
Editor: Joe Fullman, with Julia Adams

Printed in the United States of America

CPSIA compliance information: Batch #CW19GS: For further information contact Gareth Stevens, New York, New York at 1-800-542-2595.

CONTENTS

Start Experimenting! 4

Let's Get Messy! 8

The Exploding Bag 10

Fizz Fountain 12

Homemade Lava Lamp 14

Gravity Splats 16

Stream of Light 18

Slo-Mo Water Ball 20

Egg-Drop Challenge 22

Confetti Cannon 25

Odd Oobleck 27

Glossary 30

Further Information 31

Index 32

START EXPERIMENTING!

This book is packed with exciting experiments that go splat, pop, and explode, or are so incredible you won't believe your eyes! But there's nothing magical in these pages—it's all real-life amazing SCIENCE.

BE ECO-FRIENDLY!

First things first. As scientists, we aim to be as environmentally friendly as possible. Experiments require lots of different materials, including plastic ones, so we need to make sure we reuse and recycle as much as we can ...

* Some experiments use plastic straws; rather than buying a large amount, ask in coffee shops or restaurants whether they can spare a few for your experiments.

* Old cereal boxes are great for experiments that use cardboard.

* Save old school worksheets and other paper you no longer need, to reuse for experiments.

WHAT YOU'LL NEED

You can do most of these experiments with everyday items you'll find around the house.

Some useful things to have handy are ...

* Paper and cardboard

* Pens and pencils

* String

* Glue

* Tape

* Straws (plastic ones are best)

* Plates, bowls, jugs, and plastic food containers

* Scissors

* Rubber bands

* Paper cups

* Balloons

STAY SAFE!

Experiments are fun, but some of them can be dangerous if they're not done carefully ... so don't forget these safety tips:

✸ You will need an adult to help with experiments that involve cooking and heating, matches and candles, and sharp cutting tools. Wherever an experiment has something like this in it, you'll see this sign to remind you:

> ⚠ **ASK AN ADULT!**

✸ Follow all the instructions carefully to make sure you use all the equipment and materials in a safe way.

✸ If an experiment requires you to stand on a chair, make sure you have someone to assist you. Check that the chair is placed in a stable position and ask the person helping you to hold the chair while you are using it.

✱ Stand back from anything that's moving fast, or that involves eruptions or explosions. And don't throw, shoot, or whirl things around unless you're completely sure there's no one nearby.

And remember...

Always do experiments somewhere that's easy to clean up, like a kitchen or bathroom—NOT on the fancy carpet! And make sure you do clean up after yourself. Some of these experiments are messy!

So, are you ready to see some science? Step this way …

LET'S GET MESSY!

As every scientist knows, some experiments are messier than others. The experiments in this book involve gloopy slime, paint splats, messy explosions, or just getting soaking wet. Get your old clothes on!

MESSY SCIENCE
So what type of experiments make the most mess, and why?

Chemical reactions
A chemical reaction happens when two different chemicals or substances mix together and react, or change. Not all chemicals react together, but when they do, it can certainly be messy.

Messy materials
Experimenting with water, oil, eggs, paint, or other messy stuff is never going to be neat and tidy.

Explosions
We're forgetting, of course, crazy explosions that shoot everything in all directions. There are many ways to create an explosion, and you'll find a few in the following pages.

Of course, most of these extreme experiments are best done outside—or at least in a nice splatter-proof kitchen or bathroom (once you've checked with the person who owns it!).

Make a mini mess

For starters, try this simple experiment to see a basic chemical reaction at work. (Hold on to the ingredients, as you'll be needing them again soon.)

You'll need white vinegar and baking soda—both available in a supermarket.

Put a small cup or glass in a bowl, and add some vinegar to the cup or glass until it's about half full. Then get a heaping teaspoon of baking soda, and drop it in the vinegar. What happens?

HOW DOES iT WORK?

In a chemical reaction, chemicals combine and change to make new chemicals. In this experiment, the vinegar and the baking soda react to make a gas called carbon dioxide. The gas makes lots of bubbles that make the mixture foam up. The reaction also makes other chemicals. Luckily for you, they're harmless! But some reactions aren't so safe. Sometimes they can create dangerous chemicals, explosions, or flames. So always follow the instructions carefully, and don't mix the wrong things together!

THE EXPLODING BAG

This experiment reveals the true power of a chemical reaction taking place inside a plastic bag. Stand well back!

WHAT YOU'LL NEED:

* White vinegar
* Baking soda (sometimes known as bicarbonate of soda)
* Warm water
* A tablespoon
* A measuring cup or average-sized drinking cup
* A plastic food or freezer bag
* A piece of paper towel or tissue
* A big outdoor space

Some food bags have a seal that you can press tightly closed. If you don't have this type, use a large sandwich bag that you can tie a tight knot in instead.

1. Lay the piece of paper towel or tissue flat and put 2 tablespoons of baking soda into the middle.

2. Fold the paper towel up so that the powder is held safely inside, like this.

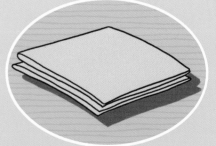

3. Put about a quarter of a cup of warm water from a hot faucet into the bag. Then add about half a cup of vinegar. Hold the bag upright so that the liquid doesn't spill out.

10

This is easier with two people— one to hold the paper towel up, the other to close the bag.

HOW DOES IT WORK?

The vinegar and baking soda react and make carbon dioxide gas (the warm water helps to speed things up). As more and more gas is made, it fills up the bag and tries to escape. Finally, the bag can't hold it in anymore, and ... SPLAT!

4. Go outside, if you aren't there already. Now put the folded-up paper towel inside the bag, but keep it away from the liquid. Seal or tie up the bag tightly so no air can escape.

5. Once the bag is sealed shut, let the paper parcel drop into the liquid. Put the bag down on the ground and wait to see what happens!

To make an even messier splat, use runny, water-based paint instead of water!

FIZZ FOUNTAIN

This famous experiment makes messy foaming cola splurt all over the place. Some versions of this experiment use candy, but salt works even better!

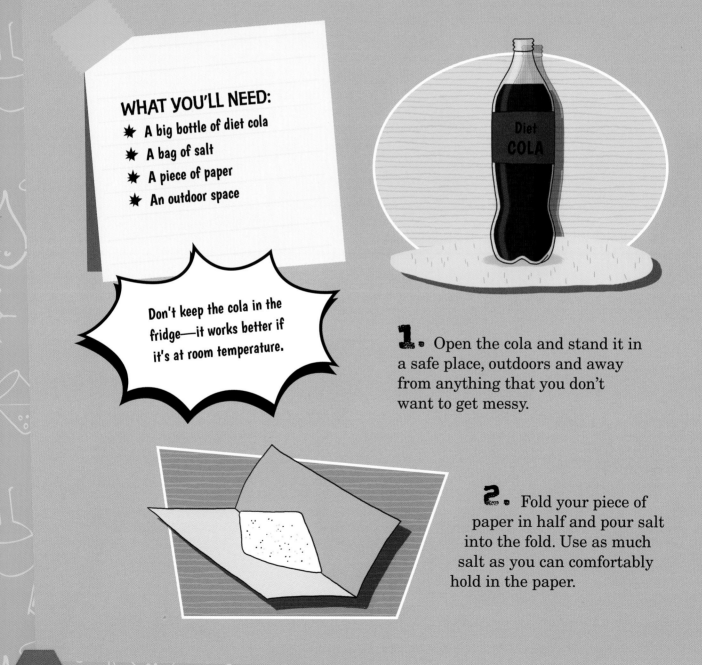

WHAT YOU'LL NEED:
* A big bottle of diet cola
* A bag of salt
* A piece of paper
* An outdoor space

Don't keep the cola in the fridge—it works better if it's at room temperature.

1. Open the cola and stand it in a safe place, outdoors and away from anything that you don't want to get messy.

2. Fold your piece of paper in half and pour salt into the fold. Use as much salt as you can comfortably hold in the paper.

3. Line up the end of the fold with the top of the bottle, then carefully tip the salt into the cola, so that it slides in quickly.

4. Stand back and watch the fountain!

HOW DOES IT WORK?

Fizzy drinks contain a lot of carbon dioxide gas, which is dissolved in the liquid. Normally, the bubbles of gas come out of the drink gradually. But the salt makes it come out much faster. Scientists think this is because the rough surfaces of the salt granules give the gas something to stick to, and it forms large bubbles. Suddenly, there's so much gas that it can't fit in the bottle, so the foamy cola shoots out.

Don't worry about having cola and salt in the same meal. An explosion only happens when a lot of salt and cola are mixed together very quickly. (Cola with chips might make you burp, though!)

HOMEMADE LAVA LAMP

A lava lamp makes bubbles of colorful hot wax float up and down inside a glass bottle. You can make your own simple version with oil, water, and food coloring.

WHAT YOU'LL NEED:

* ✷ A tall, clear container, such as a glass jar or bottle
* ✷ A bottle of sunflower oil (the type used for cooking)
* ✷ Warm water
* ✷ Liquid food coloring
* ✷ Baking powder
* ✷ A spoon

If you don't have baking powder, you could use a fizzing bath bomb broken into small pieces, or a fizzy anti-indigestion drink tablet.

1. First, pour some warm water from the hot faucet into your glass container, until it's about a quarter full. Add a few drops of food coloring in your favorite color.

2. Carefully pour in sunflower oil until the container is about three-quarters full. The liquids will swirl around, so give them a few moments to settle.

14

3. Now take a spoonful of baking powder and drop it into the container. If it sits on top of the oil at first, push it down with the spoon.

4. Watch the container from the side to see what happens.

HOW DOES IT WORK?

The baking powder contains chemicals that react with the water to make gas bubbles. The water is heavier than the oil, so the oil floats on top of it. But the bubbles are lighter, so they float to get to the top of the oil. They slowly force their way up through the oil, taking some of the colored water with them.

GRAVITY SPLATS

Use gravity to make paint splat and you can get all kinds of interesting results. It's art and science—all rolled up into one simple experiment!

WHAT YOU'LL NEED:

* ✹ Large pieces of paper, or a roll of drawing paper or plain wallpaper
* ✹ Water-based poster paint or powder paint in different colors
* ✹ Water
* ✹ Lots of plastic or paper bowls
* ✹ Rubber balls or pebbles
* ✹ Large spoons
* ✹ Old clothes and newspapers

ⓘ ASK AN ADULT!

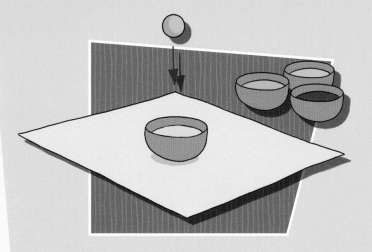

1. First, lay down newspapers to catch any mess. Then make runny paint by mixing the paint or paint powder with water in the bowls. Put a bowl of paint on the paper, then drop a rubber ball or pebble into it. Splat!

You don't have to use paper—if you have a patio, sidewalk, or playground to use, you can splat straight onto that! But make sure you get permission first.

2. Experiment with dropping the ball or pebble from a low height, and from higher up (you could stand on a chair or ask a tall adult to help). What happens to the splats?

3. For another splat method, simply get a spoonful of paint, lift it up, and tip it out onto the paper or the ground. Again, try dropping it from lower and higher up.

4. If you like, try measuring the height you drop from, and comparing this to the size of the splat you make.

If you used paper, you could let it dry, then put your splat artwork on the wall.

HOW DOES IT WORK?

Objects that are dropped from higher up make a bigger splat. Maybe that's what you expected. But why does it happen? When objects fall, they start off completely still, then speed up. The farther they fall, the faster they go. A faster object hits the ground or the paper much harder, and this forces the paint to splat out farther.

STREAM OF LIGHT

Light always travels in straight lines — or does it? In this experiment, you can make a beam of light travel along a curved stream of water.

WHAT YOU'LL NEED:
* ✸ A large, clear, plastic drink bottle
* ✸ Sharp, pointy scissors
* ✸ Water
* ✸ A large bucket, sink, or bathtub to catch the water
* ✸ A bright flashlight or laser pointer

ⓘ ASK AN ADULT!

1. Ask an adult to make a small hole, about ¼ inch (0.5 cm) across, near the bottom of the bottle. They can do this by carefully sticking the pointed tip of the scissors in and twisting it around.

2. Cover the hole with a finger, and fill the bottle to the brim with water. Stand the bottle on a flat surface next to the bucket, sink, or bathtub with the hole facing it.

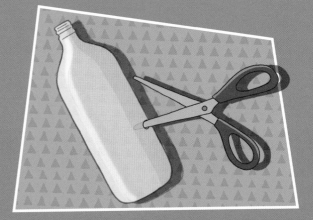

Get a friend to help you with this step.

3. Turn off the lights in the room so that you can see the flashlight light better. Switch on the flashlight or laser pointer and shine it from behind the bottle, through the water inside, and toward the hole.

HOW DOES IT WORK?

Light does travel in straight lines, but it also bounces, or reflects, off shiny surfaces. When light enters the water stream, it reflects off the inside surface of the water. It bounces to and fro inside the water stream, following its path.

4. Remove the finger and let the water flow out. You should see light flowing along the stream of water. Put your hand under it to see if it makes a spot of light on your skin.

This is the science behind fiber-optic technology, which carries light along tiny glass tubes. As light moves so fast, fiber optic cables can be used to carry lots of information in the form of light signals. They're often used as Internet cables.

SLO-MO WATER BALL

What would happen if you popped a balloon full of water on the International Space Station? This experiment might give you some idea!

WHAT YOU'LL NEED:

* ✳ A balloon
* ✳ Water
* ✳ String
* ✳ Something to hang the balloon from, such as a low tree branch or washing line
* ✳ A pin
* ✳ A smartphone or digital camera with a slow-motion filming option

1. Blow the balloon up to stretch it, then let it go down. To fill it with water, stretch the neck of the balloon over a faucet, and run the faucet slowly. You only need to fill the balloon to about half the usual size.

2. Tie the balloon closed, and tie some string around the knot. Hang the balloon up somewhere outdoors, away from anything you don't want to get wet!

3. Ask a friend to film the balloon on a slow-motion setting while you pop it (or you could set up the camera to do this by itself, using a tripod). Don't let your phone or camera get wet.

4. Once the camera is running, take the pin and gently pop the balloon. You need to do it gently so that the balloon stays as still as possible. Then play back what happened!

HOW DOES IT WORK?

Thanks to Earth's gravity, when you pop the balloon the water will soon splat all over the ground. But when you view it in slow motion, you'll see that the popped balloon shrinks away very fast, before the water has a chance to start falling. For a moment, a perfect balloon-shaped ball of water hangs in midair.

Astronauts have actually popped balloons full of water on the International Space Station. You could ask an adult to help you find a video of this on the Internet.

EGG-DROP CHALLENGE

In this "eggstreme" experiment, you have to come up with the best way to prevent a terrible mess. Can you work out how to give an egg a safe landing?

WHAT YOU'LL NEED:
* A box of eggs (not expensive ones!)
* A chair to stand on
* An outdoor space
* A selection of materials, such as straws, clear tape, cotton balls, cardboard, plastic bags, balloons, string, rubber bands

⚠ **ASK AN ADULT!**

1. Ask an adult to boil some eggs.

2. Now, stand on the chair and drop an egg onto the ground from as high in the air as you can. Crack! The egg breaks because the force of it hitting the ground cracks its shell.

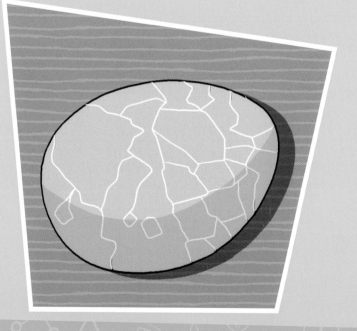

3. Your challenge is to build a wrapper, holder, or protective suit for an egg that will allow it to fall to the ground without breaking. Use the materials to try to cushion the egg or break its fall. Wrapping your egg in cotton balls might work.

4. Or perhaps you could make a protective cage for your egg using straws. If you have several people, you can all take an egg each and have a competition to see who can make the best egg protector.

If you're stuck for ideas, how about...
- A plastic-bag parachute to slow down the egg's fall
- A cushioned "airbag" made from inflated balloons or sandwich bags
- A bouncy egg hammock made from rubber bands

5. When the inventions are ready, each person can test their creation by standing on the chair and dropping their egg. Did any of the eggs survive the fall?

HOW DOES IT WORK?

Eggs have strong shells that can withstand some pressure, such as the weight of a mother hen sitting on them. However, a sudden impact will break the shell. The best way to keep the egg safe is to slow down its impact with the ground.

CONFETTI CANNON

This simple shooter made from a balloon and a cup will fire a huge burst of confetti into the air. Perfect for parties! (As long as you don't mind a massive mess, that is.)

WHAT YOU'LL NEED:
- ✹ A paper cup
- ✹ A balloon
- ✹ Scissors or a craft knife
- ✹ Clear tape
- ✹ Confetti

⚠ ASK AN ADULT!

1. Ask an adult to cut out the bottom of the paper cup using a craft knife or sharp scissors.

You can buy confetti at craft and stationery stores—or make your own by cutting colored paper or tissue paper into little pieces. You can also use a hole punch to make lots of holes in colored paper, then collect all the tiny circles that fall out.

2. Cut the round end off a balloon, and tie a knot in the neck end. Then stretch it over the bottom of your paper cup, and sticky tape it firmly in place.

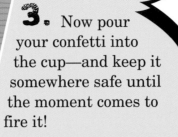

What else could you put in your cannon? Anything small and light will work—try sequins or mini craft pom-poms.

3. Now pour your confetti into the cup—and keep it somewhere safe until the moment comes to fire it!

4. When you're ready, hold the cup in one hand, and pull back the balloon with the other.

5. Then 3 … 2 … 1 … let go! Confetti should be flying through the air.

HOW DOES IT WORK?

The balloon skin is elastic and stretchy, like a rubber band. When you pull it down, it stretches, and this stores up energy. When you let go, all this energy is released at once. The balloon skin springs back up at high speed, pushing the confetti out with a bang!

ODD OOBLECK

This strange substance is named after the green slime in a book by the famous writer, Dr. Seuss. It's easy to make, but behaves in some very odd ways ...

WHAT YOU'LL NEED:

* One or more packets of cornstarch
* Water
* A measuring cup
* A large, shallow, plastic food container or mixing bowl
* Green food coloring (optional)
* Old clothes and newspaper

1. Carefully pour your cornstarch into the measuring cup to check how much you have. Then tip the cornstarch into the container.

2. Measure out half as much water as you have cornstarch. For example, if you have 2 cups (600 ml) of cornstarch, measure 1 cup (300 ml) of water. Add a few drops of food coloring if you like.

3. Add some of the water to the cornstarch and mix it with your hands. (This can take a while.) Add more water, bit by bit, until you have a gloopy, slimy mixture.

4. Now try these tests to see what the mixture does.

- Grab a handful of oobleck and squeeze it tight. Then let go and open your hand.
- Pour out a puddle of oobleck, then try to push your fingers through it quickly.
- Let a plastic toy figure sink into the oobleck as if it was quicksand, then try to pull it out quickly.

- Press your hand slowly into the oobleck—then try hitting it hard. What happens?

HOW DOES IT WORK?

Oobleck can behave like a solid or a liquid. When it's pressed hard, the ingredients lock together and it acts like a solid. But when it's handled gently, it flows like a liquid. In bigger and even messier experiments, people have filled swimming pools with oobleck and managed to run over the surface!

GLOSSARY

carbon dioxide A gas that is colorless and doesn't smell. It is a very small part of the air we breathe.

chemical reaction When two different chemicals come together and change.

dissolve To become part of a liquid.

granule A small, compact grain of something, for example sugar.

gravity A force that tries to pull two objects together. Earth's gravity is what keeps us on the ground, and what makes objects fall.

impact The action of one object forcefully coming into contact with another.

indigestion Pain in the stomach as a result of digestion difficulties.

International Space Station A space station that houses astronauts and orbits Earth.

nontoxic Not poisonous or harmful.

slo-mo Short for slow motion.

Books

Gilpin, Rebecca and Leonie Pratt. *Big Book of Science Things to Make and Do*. London, UK: Usborne Publishing, 2012.

Homer, Holly. *101 Coolest Simple Science Experiments*. Salem, MA: Page Street Publishing, 2016.

Hutchinson, Sam. *Science Activity Book*. London, UK: b small publishing, 2016.

Russell, Harriet. *This Book Thinks You're a Scientist: Imagine, Experiment, Create*. London, UK: Thames and Hudson, 2016.

Winston, Robert. *Outdoor Maker Lab*. London, UK: DK Publishing, 2018.

Websites

http://www.sciencekids.co.nz/experiments.html
A whole host of experiments that let you explore the world of science.

https://youtu.be/XtUN1rjUZRo
This video will show you how to make magnetic slime!

https://www.exploratorium.edu/snacks/subject/food-and-cooking
Discover fun, messy science experiments with food.

INDEX

art 16

balloon 5, 20, 21, 22, 23, 25, 26
boil 22
bottle 12, 13, 14, 18, 19
bubbles 9, 13, 14, 15

candy 12
carbon dioxide 9, 11, 13
chemical reaction 8, 9, 10
chemicals 8, 9, 15
cola 12, 13
confetti 25, 26

egg 8, 22, 23, 24
elastic 26
energy 26
explosion 7, 8, 9, 13

fiber-optic 19
fizz 12, 13, 14
force 15, 17, 22

gas 9, 11, 13, 15
gloop 8, 28
granule 13

gravity 16, 21

impact 24
indigestion 14
International Space Station 20, 21

lava 14
light 18, 19

mixture 9, 28, 29

nontoxic 28

oil 8, 14, 15
oobleck 27–29

paint 8, 11, 16, 17
pop 20, 21

slime 8, 27
slow motion 20, 21
speed 11, 17, 26
splat 8, 9, 11, 16, 17, 21

wax 14